PLAIN CHRISTIANITY

By J. B. Phillips

LETTERS TO YOUNG CHURCHES
   A Translation of the New Testament Epistles
THE GOSPELS translated into Modern English
YOUR GOD IS TOO SMALL
MAKING MEN WHOLE
PLAIN CHRISTIANITY and other broadcast talks

J. B. Phillips

PLAIN CHRISTIANITY

AND OTHER BROADCAST TALKS

New York

THE MACMILLAN COMPANY   1955

The quotations on pages 36 and 37 are from LETTERS TO YOUNG
CHURCHES, by J. B. Phillips, copyrighted 1947 by The Macmillan Com-
pany; on pages 80–86, from THE GOSPELS translated into Modern
English, by J. B. Phillips, copyright 1952 by The Macmillan Company.

CONTENTS

1 PLAIN CHRISTIANITY (I)   11
2 PLAIN CHRISTIANITY (II)   23
3 THE MODERN TRANSLATION OF THE NEW TESTAMENT   33
4 A GOD BIG ENOUGH   41
5 A SENSE OF SIN   49
6 WHAT IS WORSHIP?   57
7 THE HOLY SPIRIT   65
8 A THING MOST WONDERFUL   73
9 THE FIRST PORTRAIT OF JESUS   79

BY WAY OF INTRODUCTION

THE BROADCAST ADDRESSES in this small book are published in response to many requests. They are printed just as they were given, and in consequence the style is conversational and not of any literary merit. Since they were given at various times to various audiences, there is a certain amount of repetition or overlapping of ideas. The program for which each talk was designed is indicated in a note at the opening of each Address.

J. B. PHILLIPS

Redhill 1953

PLAIN CHRISTIANITY

one

PLAIN CHRISTIANITY

'PLAIN CHRISTIANITY' is what I have been asked to talk about to you and I must say I am rather glad of the title. For I am not particularly interested in religious thrills and visions (though I don't deny they have their value), but I am intensely interested in how this Christian Faith works in everyday life. Frankly, I am not a bit impressed by any religion unless it actually works out in practice; but I think the Christian religion does. In fact I do seriously think that if I were looking for the proof of the genuineness of plain Christianity, I should look first of all at the lives of the plain Christians.

Now the result of that looking may surprise you, for, in the twenty-odd years that I have been a parson, I have become more convinced of the truth of the Christian Faith by observing the lives of genuine Christians than by anything else. This thing does work out in practice. Indeed, although I believe Christianity to be historically true, that is, founded on historical facts and not on a myth or on a series of beauti-

NOTE: This talk was broadcast for the Australian Broadcasting Commission and is reproduced here by permission of the A.B.C.

ful thoughts; and although I'd be prepared to argue the value of plain Christianity as the only sane and sensible way of meeting this life and whatever lies beyond it, yet I think what convinces me most is the lives of plain Christians.

Now naturally that sounds like a very rash statement, for everyone knows there are quite a number of poor-quality Christians about who are quite the opposite of a good advertisement for their Faith. And I should have to admit, since the Christian Faith is really a way of living, that the lives of people who are trying to follow that Way are, at any given moment, at very different stages of development.

One man, for example, may have only just started to lead a Christian life, and so far only one part of his life shows any sign of improvement in quality; he may at this particular time be quite blind to what appear to us as glaring faults in other parts of his life. But I would suggest to you that just as you wouldn't judge the value of music either by the poor performer or the learner, or by bad music; and just as you wouldn't judge the value of painting by the bad painter, the mere beginner, or by bad art, so it is not really reasonable to judge the value of the Christian Faith by thinking of the hypocrites whose religion is no more than skin deep, or the beginners who have only just begun to grasp the truth, or by some caricatures of real religion which sometimes go by the name of Christianity.

No, when I talk about the lives of plain Christians as being to me a proof of the reality of the Christian Faith, I am thinking of those who have taken that Faith seriously (and by that I do not mean solemnly!), and who have over a period of years lived their lives by that Faith. As a parson I am fortunate in meeting all sorts of people of all kinds of temperament, people of varying degrees of intelligence and in various walks of life; and the thing that impresses me about the genuine Christians is a certain quality of life which they all possess. It is rather difficult to put into words and, of course, I am not claiming that they are 'saints' in the sense that they have no faults. But they all exhibit three particular characteristics which I think are quite remarkable.

The first is a kind of inward tranquillity, as though the very center of their personalities were relaxed and at peace. Many of them of course are busy people with all kinds of responsibilities to carry and often with heavy burdens to bear. But nevertheless they give me this strong impression that inside them they are at peace—and that is a thing which I very rarely see in those without a religious faith.

The second characteristic which is common to all the best Christians is an unquenchable gaiety of spirit. Christians of course never expect, and certainly don't enjoy, any particular immunity from trouble; but I find in them the ability, not only to cope courageously with their particular difficulty, but very often to cope with it good-humoredly and even joyfully. I don't want you to think that I always and invariably observe this, but I must say that I have seen it so often, and in such unlikely places, that I cannot help being very much impressed.

The third thing that I notice which is common to all Christians, whatever their background or circumstances may be, is a quality for which we can only use the word 'love.' Unfortunately, as you know, we have misused the word 'love' so many times that it has almost ceased to mean anything at all to us. But there is in the genuine Christian life not merely kindliness and charity, but what I would describe as a kind of outgoing love which really is concerned about other people. Of course there is a lot of imitation 'love' about, and since there are hypocrites among Christians as there are in any other group of people, there is unhappily such a thing as

hypocritical love—or 'love in inverted commas,' as I sometimes call it. But of course I am not talking about that, nor
am I talking about some sentimental, vague feeling of goodwill towards all mankind. The love I see exhibited in the best
Christians is a deeper thing than kindness; it is a warmer
thing than charity; and I think it is a more costly thing than
mere expressions or feelings of goodwill. In fact, it rather
looks to me as though it is some divine quality, much deeper
and more sustained than any human feeling, expressing itself
in and through normal human beings.

Now these three characteristics, which impress me very
much and which appear all over the place wherever Christianity is seriously accepted, are to my mind a very definite
pointer to something beyond merely human experience. We
all know peace of mind, when there is nothing to worry us;
we all know joy, when our surroundings are happy; and we
all know love, among our friends who love us. But the im-
pressive thing about these qualities which I have noticed
through the years is that the tranquillity exists in spite of
harassing circumstances; and the gaiety and good humor in
spite of worrying and depressing conditions; and the love is
exhibited not only in a small circle where it is likely to be
returned, but extends to places and people where it is certainly not asked for and where it may not even be appreci-
ated! To me, therefore, there is something Godlike about
these characteristics of real Christians, and I find myself
believing that they have somehow begun to share the quality
of the Life of God Himself.

Of course I can easily image the kind of thoughts that may
have been going through your minds while I have been talking. You are quite probably thinking of the nice, kind, decent,
honest people you know who make no religious pretensions
of any kind. Of course I know quite a lot of such people too.

But I do really think that there are three things which ought to be said quite kindly but firmly about good men without faith.

The first is this, that I think you will find, as I have found, that in the life history of these nice good people there has usually been genuine Christian influence. A man, for example, may grow up with no Christian faith of his own, but nevertheless with the whole of his life guided by internal principles implanted there by either one or both of his parents *who were themselves Christians.* Or sometimes you will find parents, who in their own childhood had an overdose of Church-going, bringing up their children without any form of religious faith. *But they will bring up those children according to the Christian principles which they themselves learned years ago.* This sort of phenomenon can only happen of course in a country where Christianity has been the tradition for several generations. I don't think you will find much evidence of people being naturally and spontaneously Christian where there is no Christian tradition or environment.

The second difference that I must point out between 'nice people' and Christians is that the nice people have not really in practice *enough* 'niceness.' What I mean is that they are charming and tolerant and kind within certain limits, but it is very very rare to find them coping effectively with the messes and muddles made by the sins and failures of other men. Their goodness and their love are excellent up to a point, but they do not, as with the genuine Christian, enable them to cope effectively, and indeed redemptively, with a situation that has gone badly wrong. Of course I am not claiming that all Christians invariably do deal with dark and difficult situations effectually, but I do claim that the quality of their lives is such that something makes them want to move out from their own circle of love and happiness and bear some part of the pain and cost of putting a wrong situation right. They are not always very good at it, and they by no means always succeed, but for myself I am very much impressed by the fact that they do try to do something about it. They have, as I said before, an outgoing love.

The third weakness of nice people without faith is that they have literally nothing to offer to those who are *not* nice people. They probably behave kindly and tolerantly towards selfish people, but they have no means of communicating their secret of 'niceness.' To the man who has an unpleasant background, or an inherent moral weakness, they have no gospel to offer. They cannot, as the Christian can, point to Someone stronger than themselves who is quite capable of transforming a disposition and a character. The Christian knows God, or should I say a little bit of God, through Christ, and he has learned through his own experience to tap the resources of God. He can, therefore, at least point the way to a better quality of life to someone who is not by nature a nice type or a good type or an honest type. This the good man without faith is quite unable to do, since he has no experience of the active, operative power of God.

You may think that I have been a bit hard about the nice, good, decent, kindly people who have no religious faith. I certainly don't mean to be hard on them; indeed, I am extremely grateful that there are so many such people about. But for the reasons I have given, they don't really provide much hope for a wrongheaded and sinful world. Plain Christianity on the other hand does hold out hope for every man who is prepared to believe in Christ.

The man who is a hundred per cent healthy and has never been ill in his life is not as a general rule much use in visiting the sick. It is almost impossible for him to enter into the feelings of a man who is ill. In the same way the man who is unfailingly good and generous and brave and unselfish, and all the rest of it, without much effort and without any faith, has really nothing to say to the man who knows he is by nature, and possibly through his own upbringing and circumstances, selfish and suspicious and afraid of things and people, and at the same time ashamed of himself for being afraid.

I hope you will see what I am driving at. The world is full of a kind of infection, of selfishness and fear and greed, and it isn't in the least useful simply to say, 'Why can't you be like so-and-so; he's always kind and generous and honest?' etc. But of course plain Christianity can say a great deal more than that. It does not go around denouncing men as 'sinners' but it does point to a way out.

Let us for a moment go back to the Source of the Christian religion. If you will assume for the moment what I firmly believe, that Jesus Christ was God focused in a human being, it becomes immediately immensely important to see how He dealt with the situation. He once said, with a certain irony no doubt, that He hadn't come 'to call the righteous, but sinners to change their ways.' And indeed, it is plain from the four Gospels that sinners of all kinds, that is, people who knew their lives were on the wrong track, flocked to hear Him, and many followed Him. Yet we very rarely find Him calling people sinners; what He called them to do was to 'follow' Him. Whether it was people like James and John who had a good steady fishing business, or Matthew who had built for himself a nice comfortable racket in the tax-collector's line, or whoever it was, it seems that Jesus always appealed to the real man living underneath the façade presented to the world. 'Follow Me,' He said, and that real person inside each one of them followed, sometimes, I think, to his own surprise. They found in their friendship with Him a new way of looking at Life and a new way of coping with it. Quite often, as far as we can judge, the men who followed Jesus Christ were very far from being nice decent people. Yet there was something transforming about His friendship which gave them the power to rise above their sins and become their real selves. And it is extraordinary that this transformation of human character did not cease with the physical death of Jesus. All through the New Testament records there is an altogether astonishing testimony to this power of Christ to change people from within. The call of Christ is Good News, for it brings the hope of being the-person-he-knew-he-was-always-meant-to-be to the man who is bogged down by his own failures and fears and sins.

I spoke a moment ago about Jesus Christ being God, so to speak, focused in a human being. I think unless we can accept this (the central part of the Christian Faith) we are left with thoughts of God so huge and overwhelming that He becomes quite unknowable. During the last few years Science has been discovering for us not only the immense size of the Universe, but a thousand different complexities in its working that our forefathers never dreamed of. If we even begin to imagine the kind of Mind that must be behind all the bewildering phenomena that Science observes (and several million others it has not yet observed), the idea of a Personal God becomes impossible for the mind to take in. And that is of course one reason for the kind of noncommittal agnosticism which afflicts so many modern people.

But just suppose the Christian claim is true—that a God so immeasurably vast and infinitely beyond our understanding deliberately focused Himself at a particular point in time, in the man Jesus Christ. . . . It may well sound to you an amazing thing to believe, but it isn't, surely, out of all reason.

For if God wants to make Himself known to us human beings, then it is no good overwhelming us with His greatness or His power. He must express His Character in terms that we can understand. He must reveal Himself within the limits of a human life.

Now this Man Jesus Christ once said that if a man sincerely wanted to cooperate with the plans of God, then he would know by a kind of inner endorsement whether His own teaching was a purely human invention or was in sober fact a revelation of God Himself. The actual words, which I expect you know, are: 'If any man will do his will [that is, the Father's Will], *he shall know* of the doctrine, whether it be of God, or whether I speak of myself.' Now this is exactly what happens in practice. For when a man takes this leap of faith—and that is what it is to start with—and accepts Christ as the revealed Character of God, and His teaching as the revealed Will of God, then he does find within himself this inward confirmation. The true Christian finds that, beyond all argument, he is spiritually sure; he feels, 'This is right, this is true. This is what God must be like; this is what life is meant to be.' I know that this certainty is particularly infuriating to the non-Christian, partly because it is something you cannot argue about, and partly because it only comes to those who have taken this step of faith. The agnostic who wants to sit on the fence and keep an open mind about God may retain his open mind, but he never succeeds in achieving conviction one way or the other.

I think the other obstacle between man and God which becomes apparent to any serious-minded seeker after God is the appalling gulf between God's perfection and our own sinfulness. All serious religions make some attempt, sometimes indeed most desperate and pathetic attempts, to bridge this gulf. The feeling deep in the heart of man that 'something ought to be done about it' is awakened as soon as a man begins seriously to want to approach God. I have already said that Jesus Christ did not go about underlining people's sins or trying to arouse a sense of guilt. This I think was for two reasons: first, because He knew very well that anybody who approached God would experience this sense of deep unworthiness—and of course there were people who felt it in His own presence; and secondly, because He knew that in Himself, in His own life and death and resurrection He was the Living Reconciliation between man and God. As St. Paul so rightly said, 'God was in Christ reconciling the world unto Himself.' I have not time to attempt to deal with theories of Atonement, and indeed I am not sure that the theories are important, but it is very important for us to realize that what we could never do *has been done,* by Christ. Just to accept this means a revolution in our thinking about God. For once we can see God reconciling the world unto Himself in Christ, we no longer picture Him as unimaginable Perfection inevitably and by His very nature making us feel guilty and afraid. Instead we see God stooping right down to our level, living life without supernatural advantages, but doing it perfectly. We see God Who was utter Perfection allowing the forces of evil to close in upon Him and kill Him. And we see Him passing right through death to demonstrate that in Him, the perfect human being Who was also God, death itself has no more terror.

Plain Christianity then, it seems to me, begins with accepting the claim of Jesus Christ to be God in human form. It means dropping our ridiculous habit of trying to justify ourselves and accepting the reconciliation which Christ has made. And then it means the knowledge within ourselves that we are now inseparably connected with the eternal Life of God; so that there is nothing which life can do, and nothing which death can do, to interfere with that relationship. It means, too, that since Christ is alive and well able to supply the spiritual needs of those who trust in Him, the Christian religion is no longer seen as a grim battle or a lonely, joyless pilgrimage, but as a life lived with the very vitality of God within a man—enabling him, though he may be unconscious of it, to present a quality of living which no non-Christian can produce.

Now all this is so much theory unless we really see it in practice; and that is precisely what I claim to have seen over a period of years. I find that people who accept these basic facts about God and go on maintaining their contact with Him through Christ do exhibit the qualities I have already mentioned—an inward peace, a steady joy and an overflowing love. It is possible that you who listen to me are conscious that these are the very things in which your life is deficient. It is possible, isn't it, that you have been keeping an open mind too long—you can get very tired of an open mind—and what you and I and everyone else needs is this inner spiritual quality which gives point and purpose to our living.

I don't honestly see how that is going to come to us without God, and I don't honestly see how we are going to get into contact with God without Christ. But I do assure you that where Christ's claim is accepted and where sincere adult loyalty is given to Him, the result is never a disappointment. The certainty which you may have envied in the plain Christian will become your certainty too.

~ *two*

PLAIN CHRISTIANITY (II)

THERE IS A question which I think is in a good many people's minds, though they may not often put it into words, and I am going to try to answer it. The question is simply this: 'Can I live without God?' Well, of course, the short answer to that is, 'No, of course, you can't.' The very fact that you are living at all is because you are using the very complicated mechanism which we call the body, which you had no hand in designing. You are listening to me with ears which are very delicate and complicated mechanisms, and you and I certainly had no part in making them. At the same time, you are breathing with lungs which you have never seen, you are digesting your last meal by a most complicated process which turns inanimate matter into the living cells of your body— a process about which you and I know very little. And at the same time you are using your mind in following my thoughts, and to do this you are using a brain which is an enormously complicated and highly efficient piece of apparatus. In a very real sense you could not possibly live without the One who

NOTE: This talk was broadcast for the Australian Broadcasting Commission, and is reproduced here by permission of the A.B.C.

designed and created the body you live in. I sometimes read
of certain radio or film artists who appear 'by kind permission
of Mr. So-and-so.' I may say in passing that this always
amuses me because it sounds as though the particular artist
would be invisible or inaudible unless Mr. So-and-so gave
his permission! But it is perfectly and literally true that you
and I exist at all only by kind permission of God. It is strange
how people can lose sight of this very elementary fact. Radio
construction happens to be one of my hobbies, and the other
day I was talking to a radio engineer who was pointing out
to me the finer points of a television receiver. After a bit I said
to him, 'Has it ever struck you that all this would be quite
useless if it were not for the human eye?' He paused for a
moment, then laughed and said, 'Well, to be perfectly honest,
I really hadn't thought of that.'

You see, we take the miracle of the human machine so
much for granted that we forget the Mind that must lie behind its enormously complicated design. So, I repeat, in the
strictly literal sense, *we cannot live at all without God.*

But I don't think the questioner really means the question
to be asked in just that sense. What he really means is, 'Can
I do without thinking of God, without prayer or worship, or
reading the Bible or Holy Communion? Can I live my life
without reference to God, in other words?'

Again, to give a short answer, we can say, 'Yes, you can,
millions do.' They go through life with scarcely a thought
of God from the cradle to the grave. But I believe they suffer
an immense loss in quality of living. After all, your radio
will work without an aerial, but not very well. Your car will
run on two cylinders instead of four, but not very well. If
you are a housewife you can do your cooking without ever
using sugar or salt, but neither you nor the family is going
to be pleased with the result. It seems to me it is all a question

of quality of living. You can live some sort of existence, you can get through life somehow, without any conscious reference to God, but your life is going to be of a poor quality. At the best it is going to be deficient and at the worst it is going to fall an easy prey to the various evil forces in the world. Indeed, I would go so far as to say that the reason why the world as a whole is in such a frightening mess is because the vast majority of people are living lives without God. That to my mind is not how life is meant to be lived, and humanity as a whole shows all the signs of a deficiency disease. I am convinced that we are meant to live as sons and daughters of God, and if we refuse to realize our heredity or accept it, or if we refuse to cooperate with the Will and Purpose of God, we cannot really blame Him if the human situation grows pretty appalling.

I said a few moments ago that life lived without God is of poor quality. Now that is not a favorite theory of mine. It is a conclusion based on a good deal of personal observation. I expect you've realized that a parson has an almost unique opportunity of getting to know people, people of all types and temperaments, of all classes and of varying degrees of intelligence. Not many people have that opportunity. Most people know their own circle and have only the haziest idea of how other people live, except of course through books and films. People who live in towns have very little knowledge of how country people live, and vice versa. Business people as a rule only know their business friends and acquaintances, and a few friends outside. People who work in shops get to know their own customers pretty well, but they don't have much time or opportunity for knowing many other people apart from their own friends. But people like doctors, nurses and parsons, who are allowed into the homes of all sorts of people, have, as a rule, a much wider knowledge of human nature. They are privileged really, and when they have been on the job for over twenty years, working amongst different kinds of people, they can't help noticing a difference in quality between people who have a real faith in God and people who have not. Oh, by the way, I am leaving out of this talk the hypocrites, of whom there are a few in any community, who pretend to be very holy and devout, and who are really thoroughly self-centered. I am thinking of the contrast that I have observed between the people who attempt to live without God and the people who have a living faith in Him.

Well, let us look first at the people who have no faith in God. Please remember I am not condemning them; I am just telling you what I have observed.

The first thing I notice about them is that they have not got any real purpose in life. So often they are just waiting for something—waiting for the children to grow up and be off their hands, waiting for the time when they can retire. Very rarely have they got any sense of joining in and helping with a Purpose bigger than themselves. Many of them are very nice kindly people, but if you ask them straight out: 'What are you living for?' they can usually give you only the most hazy or most trivial answers. I don't think they are aware of it, but to me it is pathetically clear that they are not linked to anything or anyone bigger than themselves.

In the second place I notice that such people have no one and nothing to turn to when they reach the end of their own resources. For example, a man may be cursed with a bad temper. He may know perfectly well that it worries his wife and frightens his children and spoils the atmosphere of his home. When he is pretty young he may battle against it and sometimes succeed, but as time goes on and he is defeated more often than not, he is very apt to conclude that there is nothing that can be done about it. His bad temper, or whatever the fault may be, is just one of those things that can't be altered. And so he shrugs his shoulders and simply makes a compromise with the bad temper or the jealous spirit or the bitter tongue, or whatever else it is that is spoiling his life. He does not know of any source to which he can turn which can enable him to control his own nature, still less to transform it.

Then too, I have noticed again and again that people who live without God are all right as long as they are well and reasonably prosperous, but that illness or accident knocks them completely sideways. Oh, they are ready enough then with, 'How can there be a God to allow this to happen to me?' But they have never learned to find God as a refuge and a strength in good times as well as bad. Many of them are remarkably brave, but many more are completely lost when, for example, health fails, or there is some tragic happening in the family. They have literally no one to whom to turn.

The third thing that I notice about people who live without God, which I think I mentioned when I last spoke to you on this Program, is that they have nothing constructive to offer to the men or women who are defeated either by their own natures or by the circumstances of life. Of course, they can and do say things like: 'Cheer up—it may not be as bad as you think' or 'Pull yourself together' or even, 'Why can't you be like me?' but what they can never say, what they are quite unable to say, is 'I know Someone who is far stronger than you or I, who has helped me and who can help you.' In other words, because they have no experience of God, they have no experience of any power or resource or refuge or strength outside themselves. And I think that is a very impoverishing thing.

Now may I tell you what I have observed of the quality

of the life of the Christians that I have known? Naturally I
have known a lot in the twenty-odd years that I have been
a parson, and as far as outward circumstances, gifts and
temperaments go, they have been a very varied bunch of
people. Nevertheless, I am left with a very strong impression
of a better quality of life lived by these people who have faith
in God. I certainly don't mean that they are all perfect, or
even that they are all saintly in the commonly accepted sense
of that term. But, though they may be unaware of it themselves, their lives have got a quality—yes, I would almost call
it a superhuman quality—which people who try to live without God never possess. There are many ways in which this
shows itself, and I am only going to mention briefly four of
them.

First, I notice that Christian men and women with a living
faith in the living God have learned how the power of God
can help them to cope with their own difficult natures. I don't
claim that they always succeed, but I do claim that they
know where to turn for spiritual reinforcement, and I do
claim that in most of them you can easily detect something,
or perhaps I should say Someone, operating in their own
personalities who is higher and better than they would be by
themselves. To put it quite bluntly, I have known people
who would be called what we popularly term 'nasty bits of
work' if there were not operating in them Someone making
them into good bits of work—changing them in fact into
sons and daughters of God. Even allowing for the failures, it
is to me one of the biggest arguments for the existence of
God that I see Him operating in lives which are open to Him.
I am not speaking of the superpious, but of the ordinary
people who are open on the God-ward side and to whom
marriage or home life or business life has been made of quite
a different quality by the unseen Spirit of God.

In the second place I notice that real Christian people have as a rule much more concern and much more love for those outside their immediate circle. People living without God are friendly towards those who are friendly with them, of course, but usually their friendliness and concern only operate within a very restricted circle. But when a man opens his life to God, something of the Love of God comes into his heart, and his sympathies grow both wider and deeper. This is only perhaps what you might expect since God loves every man, but it is wonderful to see how Christian people can give time and money and a very real love to those who are quite outside their ordinary circle of acquaintances. It may be that they have a special concern for the blind or other incapacitated people. It may be that they have a special concern for those who have never heard the Gospel of Jesus Christ. But the real point is that they have a concern for the well-being of others, and I find this very well marked in all true Christians.

The third thing that I must say about Christian people is something in the nature of a tribute. Christians do not, as some people foolishly suppose, imagine that they are specially protected from life's ills and accidents, from sickness, bereavement, anxiety and all the rest. Indeed, it sometimes looks as though some of the very best people get far more than their share of misfortune. And yet I can't help observing (and this is where I pay my tribute), that these grand people can bear disappointment and loss and ill-health and all the other things that get people down, not only without bitterness but with the most astonishing courage and good humor. Again, I don't wish to make extravagant claims. They don't all do this. But I have seen so many of them living out the truth of St. Paul's words, 'In all these things we are more than conquerors,' that I am most profoundly moved and impressed. You see, theirs is not just a defiant courage, but that miraculous brave acceptance of the situation that turns a thing which is in itself evil into a shining beacon of faith and light and courage. Such grand Christians—and, thank God, I have met many of them—give the rest of us enormous encouragement.

The last thing I would say about people who live their lives with faith in God is that they have a Gospel to pass on. Many of them may be quite rightly reticent about their faith, for after all it is the most intimate side of their lives. But when the opportunity and the need arise, they can and do say something like this: 'I know Someone far greater and stronger than you or I, Someone who has helped me through some pretty rough patches, and I am sure He can help you.' And then sometimes they are able to show someone else, who up till now has lived life without God, how it is possible to get to know the infinite God through Christ, and how it is possible to tap His boundless resources through His Spirit who is living and active today.

I feel sure you must see, even if you don't agree with me, that I cannot possibly lightly dismiss from my mind what I have actually observed; the difference in quality between the people without God and the people with God is so marked that no honest man can lightly dismiss it.

It is possible that someone listening to me today has up till now been living life without God. It is possible that you feel in your bones that there is a life of a better quality, a more satisfying quality for you. You may want to feel part of a big Purpose, you may want to know that you are linked with your heavenly Father, you may even be a little tired of the sterility of life bounded by the limits of this little world. Can you live without God? Well, of course, you can, but why should you? God offers you, as your New Testament will tell you, fellowship with Himself, full and free forgiveness for the past, more than sufficient power for the present, and the future. He offers you a share as cooperator in His vast Plan, and He offers you a share in that timeless life of His which is unaffected by what we call death. You have only to accept these things as God's free gift (for that is what they are), and your life too will begin to change in quality. You will no longer live as a unit of the human race, a more or less disgruntled specimen of *homo sapiens*, you will begin to realize what you were born for; you will begin to live as a son or a daughter of God.

three

THE MODERN TRANSLATION
OF THE NEW TESTAMENT

WHEN I WAS a small boy I used to love reading a book called *The Swiss Family Robinson*. It was not until years later that I realized that I'd been reading a translation. A few years ago I read two books by that farsighted Russian theologian, Nicolas Berdyaev, and I have to admit that it was some little time before somebody told me that Berdyaev didn't write in English at all! Again, I was reading a translation without knowing it.

To my mind one of the tests of a real translation lies just here: that if the work is skillfully done, we have no idea that we're not reading the original. The thoughts, the feelings, even something of the atmosphere and the style have been carried over from one language into another. As everyone knows, translation means the act of carrying over, and we have in the Anglican Church a rather amusing survival of its use applied to people instead of merely to words. A Bishop is 'translated' from one diocese to another to this very day. I

NOTE: This talk was broadcast for the Australian Broadcasting Commission and is reproduced here by permission of the A.B.C.

think in a way, with all due respect to the Bishops, their 'translation' is a very good example of what real translation should be. For when the Bishop of X—— is translated to the Diocese of Y—— he remains the same man. His personality, his character, his qualities of mind and spirit remain exactly the same, though it's quite true that after his translation, since Y—— may be a very different diocese from X——, he may have to modify or change some of his methods and activities. But on the other hand, when Shakespeare says, 'Bless thee, Bottom, bless thee! Thou art translated,' it is pretty clear that he means something very different—he means changed in form and appearance, almost beyond recognition. And that, of course, is what bad translation does to literature.

Unfortunately, when we come to translating the New Testament, real translation becomes almost impossible for various reasons, of which I will mention only two. The first is that, although not very many people nowadays hold what we might call a mechanical view of the inspiration of the Scriptures—that is, that they were dictated from Heaven word by word to the sacred writers—yet there remains such a tremendous reverence for the Word of God and especially for what may have been the actual words of Christ, that people tend to look with disfavor upon the translator who does anything more than substitute for any Greek word its nearest English equivalent. Yet if he's really to *translate*, to carry over the meaning, and the spirit, of the original, he must have the same freedom in his use of words as he'd have in translating any other book from an ancient tongue into modern English.

The second reason why real translation is so difficult is this: that the very beauty and majesty of the Authorized Version have so permeated our minds, consciously and unconsciously, that we find it irritating and distasteful to hear the lovely cadences and majestic rhythms discarded in favor of everyday speech. I yield to no one in my profound admiration of, and thankfulness for the matchless beauty of the Authorized Version, but it's very necessary to remind ourselves that this beauty is no more a part of the original writing than is the scarlet and blue and gold decoration of the medieval manuscripts. People find it very hard to believe this, but it is undeniable that our New Testament manuscripts are written in a Greek which had long since lost its classical beauty; it was a language whose chief value lay in the fact that it was widely understood.

Innumerable papyri have been discovered in Egypt written in this same Koine, the common Greek language of the time, containing such things as descriptions of land, receipts for money, and even laundry lists! These discoveries have of course shed considerable light on the meaning of the Greek of the New Testament, but they certainly serve to underline the fact that in the providence of God His Word in the New Testament was written, not in a language of superb beauty, but in a language which the greatest number of people would be able to understand. It's not altogether easy for us to accept this, especially if we're steeped in the English of the Authorized Version, but when we do see it, we realize that it's all part of that astonishing, that breath-taking, humility of God whose Son was born in a stable and who worked in a carpenter's shop.

The translator then of the New Testament must free himself by a deliberate act of will, for a time, from his familiarity with the Authorized Version. He must soak himself, as it were, in the language of the book before him. Not only must he use the utmost care and every ounce of skill that he possesses to carry over the meaning and 'feel' of the matter before him, but he must use his imagination and put himself into the shoes of the person who is writing. If he's translating St. Paul, he must *be* St. Paul for the time being, and he must strive to create in the minds of his readers today the same sort of impression as that which St. Paul aroused in the minds of his readers nearly two thousand years ago. This at once poses a difficulty, for these are ancient letters, written in ancient times, to people long ago departed this life. The translator has to make up his mind whether he's going to try to create a sort of 'antique' atmosphere, suggesting that these were inspired writings of long ago; or whether he's going to try to short-circuit the passage of time and write these Letters or Gospels, as the case may be, as though they were written only a week or two ago. For myself I've chosen the latter course, partly because I believe very firmly in the inspiration of the New Testament and that it is full of meaning and relevance for us today; and partly because, to be frank, I found these ancient writings so alive in the hand, so to speak, that it was not nearly so difficult as it sounds to put oneself imaginatively in the place of the original writers. For example, it's not really very difficult if you closely study the writings of St. Paul to feel something of what he felt when he wrote what we know as the Second Epistle to the Corinthians.

Here is a short quotation from that Epistle (7:2–4):

Do make room in your hearts again for us! Not one of you has ever been wronged or ruined or cheated by us. I don't say this to condemn your attitude, but simply because, as I said before, whether we live or die you live in our hearts. To your face I talk to you with utter frankness; behind your back I talk about you with deepest pride. Whatever troubles I have gone through, the thought of you has filled me with comfort and deep happiness.

One of the temptations which beset a translator is to give his translation a twist according to some particular bee in his own bonnet. I think he should be extremely firm with himself over this, for of course he has no right, however strong his feelings may be, to construe a passage according to his own liking. Indeed, to be perfectly frank, there are times when a translator wishes that the material before him were capable of a slightly different translation. 'How much better that would sound, and how much more I should like it,' he sometimes feels, 'if only the Greek said that!' But what the best scholars have decided is the most reliable text is for the translator absolutely sacred. He must never read back into it what he would like it to mean. And yet I know in my own experience, which I've no doubt is similar to that of other translators, that one is accused sometimes of doing this very thing! In defence of translators, I must point out that the scholars, the experts on textual criticism, and the experts on meanings of a word, by no means always agree, and the translator, after possibly an agony of indecision, has got to come down on one side of the fence or the other. Perhaps I may take a very simple example where, through their lack of capital letters for the pronouns referring to God, both the Authorized Version and the Revised Version can escape responsibility. What, for example, are we to make of 1 John 3:9, which reads in the Authorized Version:

Whosoever is born of God doth not commit sin; for *his* seed remaineth in *him*.

Should either or both the 'his' and 'him' have a capital H? The modern translator who uses capital letters must make up his mind, he cannot avoid the issue, and for myself I have translated like this:

The man who is really God's son does not practise sin, for God's nature is in him, for good, and such a heredity is incapable of sin.

Again, the modern translator who uses quotation marks for speech has to decide where the recorded speech ends and the narrator resumes. The third chapter in John is a case in point. Did *Jesus* say the famous words in the sixteenth verse: 'God so loved the world . . .' or are they the comment of St. John? Nobody knows. But in this and a hundred other cases the modern translator, after the most careful consideration, has got to decide one way or the other.

Translation, as I see it, and as I have attempted it, is very far from being a matter of putting English equivalents for Greek words, even though the discovery of the Egyptian papyri has made the meaning of some of those words more clear and definite. To set about the task that way leads straight to Translator's English—that horrible mixture of ancient and modern which has never been spoken or written in any country at any time. No, the task is much more exacting than that. It is the attempt to re-create in the mind and soul of the modern reader a similar reaction to that created in those who first read these inspired words. No translator faced with this formidable task would claim to have succeeded more than partially. And he knows he runs the gantlet, both of those who are wedded to the peerless beauty of the Authorized Version, and of those who suppose that to translate into modern English is merely a matter of easy paraphrase. But his soul is encouraged and he thanks God most sincerely when the light of God's Word shines through the simple modern dress, and people say, 'I have understood so-and-so for the first time in my life.' I would like now to quote three instances from my own translation which may throw some light on the remarks which I have made:

Number one is from the second verse of St. Matthew, chapter 6. Here we know from the receipts among the Egyptian papyri that the verb ἀπεχέσθαι is used to mean 'paid in full.' So that we can now translate the comment of Jesus when He speaks scathingly of those who do their deeds of charity in public like this: 'Believe me, they have had all the reward they are going to get.'

The second example comes from the first verse of St. John's Gospel: 'In the beginning was the Word.' Now all those who are students of the New Testament will know that Logos, translated 'Word,' was a philosophical term in common use among the Jews at Alexandria (and probably among the educated elsewhere). But the ordinary man of today knows nothing of this. Yet he certainly knows that a 'word' is an outward expression of an inward thought. I have therefore translated the famous passage like this: 'At the beginning God expressed Himself. That Personal Expression was with God and was God, and He existed with God from the beginning.'

The third example comes in St. Luke, chapter 24, in that most beautiful and moving story of the walk to Emmaus. In verse thirty, we get the word ἐγένετο, translated in the Authorized Version, 'And it came to pass,' placed emphatically at the beginning of a sentence. You may think it is a mere journalistic trick, but I have turned this into a separate sentence and printed it in italics. It runs like this: *'Then it happened!* While He was sitting at table with them He took the loaf, gave thanks, broke it and passed it to them. Their eyes opened wide and *they knew Him!'* I feel this is quite justifiable, for this is exactly how we in our modern speech throw particular emphasis upon a word, as St. Luke did with καὶ ἐγένετο long ago.

No modern translator, and certainly not myself, is in any sense in competition with the Authorized Version that you know so well. What we're trying to do by the help of God and by such skill and imagination as He has given us, is to give you in English as nearly and as accurately as we can what was written twenty centuries ago. 'It's like seeing a famous picture after it's been cleaned,' a well known English scholar once wrote to me. I treasure those words, for although I know that there will always be those who prefer the mellow patina of age, there are those who are willing and indeed eager to read a conscientious attempt to bring across the centuries the inspired words in all their vividness, directness and lack of decoration.

⌁ four

A GOD BIG ENOUGH

I WANT TO talk to you about something rather personal and I hope you won't mind. It's about what you think God's like.

You see, parsons meet a good many people and hear a lot of confidences, and if my own experience is anything to go by I should say that quite a number of people have got much too small an idea of God. Perhaps you yourself had a fairly clear idea of God when you were a child and went to Sunday School, but now that you're grown up you feel that you've left all that behind. That idea of yours was all right for a child, but it doesn't satisfy you, in fact it doesn't even interest you as a grown-up man or woman. I quite agree. But I wish I could make you see that what has happened is not that you've outgrown Christianity but simply that you've outgrown your childish ideas of it. Most people develop a great deal physically, mentally and psychologically as they grow up. They learn their job and can cope with all kinds of difficult problems, but *as far as religion is concerned a lot of them haven't grown up at all.* They haven't given it anything like the thought and attention that they've given to

NOTE: This talk was broadcast in the People's Service on the Light Program of the B.B.C.

41

their jobs, or even their football pools. So we can't be surprised to find that their ideas about God are too small and childish. Naturally you don't want to love or worship or serve a God that you've outgrown!

What bothers me is that you're probably thinking that we parsons and our fellow Christians are still trying to worship and serve a childish God like that.

We're not doing anything of the kind, really, but as long as you think that I suppose you can't help thinking of us—however nice you may be about it—as rather sentimental saps who don't know the hard facts of everyday life. And, of course, you don't see any reason why you should join with us in what we are trying to do, if that's how you feel about it.

Well, I don't want to be rude, but I'd say to you—'It's about time you began to get a few grown-up ideas about God.' We sometimes say to people, 'Be your age!' or even more bluntly, 'Wise up!' Well, you've got to do both these things if you're to have a God big enough to command the loyalty of a grown-up person.

Once in London during the war I asked a group of young people if they would answer a question quickly, without reflection. 'O. K.,' they said. 'The question,' I said, 'is this: Do you think God understands radar?' They all said 'No,' and then, of course, roared with laughter as they realized how ridiculous the answer was! But the 'snap answer' showed me what I suspected—*that at the back of their minds* there was an idea of God as an old gentleman who lived in the past and was rather bewildered by modern progress.

I'm quite sure a lot of people today have got, in the back of their minds, maybe, some such ridiculous ideas of God. I suggest that we bring these ideas to the surface, and have a good critical look at them, and see if they are anything like 'big' enough for the living God of today. Some of the ideas that people have are merely quaint and simple, but some of them are tragic caricatures. How *can* you love God if in your heart of hearts you think He's a Spoilsport or a Tyrant or a Dreadful Judge or a sort of Superpoliceman? Yet I know that some good, well meaning people are trying hard to love a God who is just completely unlovable, and is supposed to do things that we should despise if a human being did them.

Of course, there's the other side. There are people who have taught their own consciences never to come between them and what they want. There are people who are so out of touch with spiritual truth that God to them is no more than a vague benevolence with about as much moral authority as Father Christmas! These people, too, ought to begin to use their minds like grown-up people. Of course, you won't have the slightest reverence for a God made in the image of Father Christmas, or any wish to love and serve Him!

Then there are the people who try to confine God within a sort of box of their own making. They need to think very hard—that God is not Episcopalian or Baptist or Methodist— or English, or even the God of this world alone. Once you see the 'bigness' of God and see the attempt to confine Him to one particular group of Christians or one particular race you don't know whether to laugh or cry. You're probably wise to do both.

Yes, even those of us who profess and call ourselves Christians need to beware of having a view of God that's too small. We have to beware of confining God to the pages of the Bible (though He certainly does speak there) or to the four walls of a Church (though He certainly is present there). I sometimes think the pictures in our Prayer books, instead of being reproductions of religious works of art, should be, for instance, a picture of the Milky Way—to remind us of the vastness of God's Creation; a picture of a bowl of flowers—to remind us of His love of beauty; even a picture of the structure of the human eye—to remind us of His meticulous accuracy as Designer.

And so, if we're going to get to know God the first step for a great many of us today is to clean up our ideas about Him. We must bring to the surface of our minds all the false and inadequate ideas—and see how false and inadequate they are. We must use our adult minds or we shall go through life thinking that God is a childish fancy and no more.

Having done this, I would suggest that we open every door of our minds and spirits to let in the bigness of God. We need to associate with God all that is lovely and wonderful and mysterious and heart-warming. We can go on and on at this. We can never have too big an idea of God.

I've tried to show how important it is to have a big enough idea of God. But perhaps you feel like butting in at this point and saying, 'Yes, but the real truth is that God is *too* big, too impersonal.' We can connect up with God in our minds all that we know of goodness and truth and beauty and mystery and wonder, and still find Him impersonal and unapproachable. What has happened then is that we are beginning to get a big idea of God but it is *unfocused and vague*—rather like looking at the moon through a telescope that's not properly focused.

What we human beings really need, if we're ever to know God at all, is to see Him 'focused' in a form that we can understand. He must 'speak our language,' as it were, if we're ever to have a hope of understanding the Character of Anyone so vast and so complex.

This is exactly what He has done. God did deliberately focus Himself in a human being when He became a man in Jesus Christ. 'The word became flesh,' wrote St. John long ago; which is another way of saying that God expressed Himself in a human being.

It is, of course, a terrific thing to believe. I haven't much use for people who say, 'Oh, you mean the Incarnation,' and let it go at that. It doesn't seem as if they'd really sat down and thought what a staggering thing it is to believe that God in all His greatness and wisdom and splendor should deliberately stoop to become a human baby. I confess it takes my breath away.

But once you do believe it, really believe it, two rather wonderful things happen. First, you know now by looking at Jesus Christ what the eternal God is really like. You can read in the Gospels and understand for yourself what He is trying to do in this world, and what sort of people He wants us to become. You can begin to see the meaning behind the plain and obvious happenings of everyday life. In fact, once you accept Jesus Christ as the true Character of God expressed in human history you can begin to learn the *real* 'facts of life.'

The second wonderful thing that happens when you take this step (and of course this always makes the critics of Christianity go purple in the face!) is that you know that this is *right*. To quote St. John again, 'He that believeth that Jesus is the Son of God hath the witness in himself.' In other words, once you accept this amazing Act of God as true, something in you 'clicks over,' like the right key turning in the lock. You just *know* that here is the Way In. This is the way that leads you to understand what life is all about, this is the way that leads you to become your real self, and this is the way that leads you to know the true and living God.

I know that this certainty which Christians claim to have

makes our opponents furiously angry, but I have seen it so many times in other people that, quite apart from my own experience, I know it is a fact.

This too is a fact; that I have never yet met anyone with a real certainty about God who did not accept this focusing of God in the Man Jesus Christ. I have known, and do know, quite a lot of clever people to whom Christianity is a myth. *But they don't know God.* On the other hand I know hundreds of people, clever and stupid, rich and poor, old and young, who have accepted the great Fact *and are sure of God.* That to me is evidence that can't be disregarded.

But now I imagine some of you, who've been listening very critically, saying: 'Look here, you're contradicting yourself, First you say, "Away with all the little old-fashioned stuffy ideas of God. Fling the windows of mind and spirit wide!" and then in the very next breath you say that "the only way to know that immensely complex Intelligence that we call God is through the Man Jesus Christ, who lived in Palestine 1900 years ago!" ' But that isn't really a contradiction, you know, though it would be if the man Jesus had been merely a figure of history. But He isn't. Christians are not worshiping and loving and serving someone who died a long time ago, but someone who is alive today. That's the whole point, and the most important thing of all. Christ is alive and immensely active today.

I would recommend you to read the New Testament with an adult, critical mind. (That's something, by the way, that thousands of people today have never done.) You will find in the character of Jesus nothing less than God, showing Himself as a human being at a particular time and in a particular country, and giving us authentic information about life, that we should be lost without. But—here's the point I'm trying to stress—that Character once shown to us in history, is still alive today. Not only above us, infinitely above us in wisdom and love and understanding, but also *with* us in the here and now, in all the strains and stresses and problems of life on this planet in the present year.

The 'way in' for us human beings is through God-become-Man, Jesus Christ. Without Him we either make ourselves silly little artificial gods which have no real effect on the way we live or else we feel stunned and awed and bewildered at the baffling mystery of that tremendous Power we call God, without knowing what we mean by it. But with Christ we can begin to understand. With Him we can begin to see what it's all about. With Him we can begin to cooperate. With Him we can lose our loneliness and feel that this immense God is really and truly our Father.

But what a God! To be willing to come down from the incredible heights of His wisdom and power and become one of us—just so that we might see what He is like and learn to know Him! Once you see that, you feel that nothing is too much to do for Him!

∼ five

A SENSE OF SIN

I FEEL PRETTY certain there are nearly as many wrong ideas about 'sin' as there are false ideas of God.

I should like to say straight out that I sympathize rather strongly with the man who says 'I don't feel a "miserable sinner" so why should I come to Church and say that I am one?' I also sympathize with the people who feel that the Christian religion is often rather morbidly preoccupied with the matter of sin.

Now please don't jump to the conclusion that here's a parson who doesn't believe there's such a thing as sin, or thinks it doesn't matter! That wouldn't be true a bit. But I do think that a lot of people have been made to feel guilty in a quite artificial way. And I do think that a lot of people have no sense of sin at all because they've managed, so far, to keep God at arm's length. I am all *for* a *real* sense of sin, as I hope to show presently. But I'm dead against people saying they're sinners merely because they think they ought to.

NOTE: This talk was broadcast in the People's Service on the Light Program of the B.B.C.

49

And I must say I get really angry with people who deliberately set out to make other people feel guilty.

Let us look for a moment at Jesus Christ. He was, I believe, God in human form, and to say that we should study His methods with the deepest respect is to put it mildly. What do we find? We find that only very rarely did He call people sinners, and never, as far as I can see, did He deliberately set out to arouse a feeling of guilt. In fact (and perhaps I ought to whisper this!) it was the *religious*, self-righteous people whom He treated in that way. But with the ordinary run of people Christ did not start by trying to arouse a sense of sin. He called men to follow Him, to help Him build the Kingdom of God on earth, where God should be Father and all men brothers. He called men to leave their self-centeredness and being so busy themselves. He called them to put God first and the good of their neighbors second, whatever the risk or the cost might be.

Of course He couldn't help arousing a *genuine* sense of sin. You can't have Light coming into a dark and dirty room without showing up the muddle and mess and dirt! The very presence of one Good Man was bound to show up the weakness and selfishness and sin of the others. But there was nothing morbid about it. There's nothing morbid about it when the doctor tells you what's wrong with you and how you can get better. It's a relief—and there's hope and health in knowing the facts. What *is* morbid is to conceal what's wrong and pretend there's nothing the matter. Truth may hurt but it cannot harm. So it was with Christ. As men got to know Him and tried to follow His new way of living which was based on love for God and your neighbor instead of on self-interest, they pretty soon found out their own sins and weaknesses. In fact, without any morbid groveling or introspection, they felt a genuine sense of sin and a genuine need of forgiveness. That, to my mind, is miles away from being deliberately made to feel a 'miserable sinner.'

In that delightful children's book by Kenneth Grahame called *The Wind in the Willows*, there are various animals in the story with very human characteristics. There's Toad, a frightfully conceited chap who loves to rush all over the country in a car and is always singing his own praises. Well, Toad gets into a frightful mess through his conceit and selfishness, and eventually his friends Mole and Rat get Badger, who is a rather stern and unbending type, to give him a good talking-to. In Badger's smoking room Toad breaks down completely, admits all his folly and guilt, sobs out his repentance and promises complete reform. So Badger lets him go, apparently a reformed character.

But a very few minutes later *outside* the smoking room we find Toad chucking his weight about just as before! Rat and Mole are horrified. 'What?' cries Badger. 'You backsliding animal, didn't you tell me just now, in there——' 'Oh yes, yes, in *there*,' says Toad impatiently, 'I'd have said anything in *there*. But I've been searching my mind since, and I find I'm not a bit sorry or repentant really, so it's no earthly good saying I am: now, is it?'

I have often thought that this is a perfect example of a false sense of sin. It doesn't matter whether it's Badger in a story, or a parent or teacher or parson in real life—if you try to make people feel a sense of sin, it won't last . . . it may even produce the opposite effect to the one you want! In my twenty-odd years as a parson I've heard a lot of confidences from people who have been *made* to feel guilty. Under the pressure of someone else's personality they may have admitted and promised all sorts of things. The tragedy is that some of them thought that such artificial guilt injection *was* the Christian faith. And, of course, in later years when they're free of that false feeling they want nothing more to do with Christianity. Can you wonder?

The method of Jesus Christ, who is alive today, remember, is very different. He calls to you to follow Him and the way of life He taught. I don't believe there's any dodging that call, and if you keep it at arm's length for years, sooner or later it will face you. For He was Reality, and there's no evading Reality.

Now it is true that we who are trying to follow Him today do find that we are, in sober fact, sinners. There never was a Christian yet who didn't reach the point of seeing that. But you can't *force* it on people. It's no good for me or anybody else to thunder at you that you're a sinner! It's a thing you've got to find out for yourself.

Some people have it brought home to them when they suddenly see the harm their selfish living has done to others. Some who take the trouble to study Christ's teaching see the appalling difference between what they *are* and what God is plainly trying to make them *become*, and that shakes them. Some feel their own sin when they're in contact with someone who is really good—not goody-goody or pious, but just solid *good*. It may make you feel a worm, it may make you feel what a conceited ass you've been. And, of course, it may make you laugh and light a cigarette and switch off this program.

But don't let's get melodramatic or morbid or self-pitying about it. If you begin to follow God instead of going your own sweet way there's bound to be a moment—and probably more than one—when you feel cheap and nasty. Don't worry, that's a good healthy sign. It means you're beginning to touch reality!

But please don't think for a moment that it gives God any pleasure to make you feel sinful, or to humiliate you. God is much too big a person for that. But once you've seen a bit of the real God in Jesus Christ and have started to cooperate with what He shows you to be His plan, I'm afraid you're bound to feel soiled and flabby and a bit of a fool. But don't worry. God can put all that straight: after all, He's the only One who has the right to forgive.

Do try to see how we human beings, who are so infected by our own and other people's sin and selfishness, do *need* to be reconciled to God who is Absolute Perfection. Of course, if you're still thinking of God as a sort of magnified Father Christmas you won't see the point. But all the great religions of the world, and everyone who has thought seriously about religion, recognizes the problem. It's roughly this. If God is sheer absolute Goodness, a sort of fire of Love and Truth, He must mean destruction to all that is false and evil. Light destroys darkness and a disinfectant destroys germs, not because they are annoyed about it but because it is their nature to do so. The blazing moral Perfection of God is certain death to evil, not because God is, like some Superman, in a furious temper, but because it is His nature. The problem is, and has always been, how can man safely approach the unimaginable Perfection of God?

Practically all religions offer some sort of 'bridgehead' towards God . . . to try to get over this truly alarming situation. We may feel sorry for primitive tribes who make animal sacrifices, we may smile tolerantly at the man who lies on a bed of spikes, or we may laugh off the whole business of trying to get right with God as mere superstition. But very deep in our natures, overlaid with all the cushions of civilization, is our own feeling that 'something ought to be done about it.' We know very well that there's got to be some sort of reconciliation between us and God.

Of course we keep this well hidden. We comfort ourselves

by saying, 'Well, I'm not as bad as so-and-so.' We even cheer
ourselves up by reading certain spicy bits in the Sunday
newspapers and congratulate ourselves that we're not as bad
as that.

But none of this solves the problem. The plain blunt fact
is that we can do nothing to manufacture a safe approach
to God. Of course, so long as we're *here* in this world and
have got good health and reasonable income we can kid
ourselves along. But what about *there*—in His perfect world
—where there's not a scrap of cover, and all our convenient
powers of forgetting the rotten things we've done have dis-
appeared? It makes you think, doesn't it?

But fortunately God knows all about this, and every other
problem. Fortunately He loves us very deeply and truly. So
much so that He came personally to this planet to deal with
this problem of bridging the gulf. He did not come to condemn but to save. He came to offer a Way out of the sin-
fear-death complex in which the world is involved.

I wonder if I can make His method clear? I don't think it's
easy to put it in a few words. But let's try. It was something
like this.

God, incredible as it may seem, entered this world as a
human being in Christ. He showed men the Character of
God, and He outlined the methods of real, full, happy living.
And then, He allowed the forces of evil—jealousy, spite,
greed, lust for power and all the rest—to close in on Him and
kill Him. I don't think you and I can begin to understand
the sort of repulsion that He must have felt as this happened
to Him. But I think He saw it as the only way out of the
impossible situation into which men were jammed. He, God,
as a Human Being, as the Representative Human Being, must
take the rap! It happened to have been a crucifixion, but it
might just as well have happened in a gas chamber or an

electric chair. Because it was God doing it the time and place don't matter. It was done deliberately as an act of reconciliation on God's part. Everyone who stops trying to 'put up a case,' or to justify themselves, and accepts this terrific Act of God finds the gulf is bridged! The feeling that 'something ought to be done about it' is miraculously set at rest. The fear of God is replaced by a deep sense of gratitude.

I can't explain this, even if there were time. I just know that it's a fact of experience. For nineteen centuries people in all parts of the world have found the love of God convincingly demonstrated in the death of Christ on the Cross. 'God was in Christ, reconciling the world unto Himself,' wrote St. Paul, and millions have endorsed his words. You don't have to earn forgiveness (how can you, anyway?) but it's there if you'll accept it.

It's difficult to avoid loving a God who acts like that. You can feel resentful and rebellious against a Moral Perfection who exists far beyond us and is not exposed to any of our dangers and temptations. But think for a moment of God stripped of all His power and majesty, down in the sweat and dust and agony of human living. Think of Him at the last refusing to accept a celestial rescue party so that He might demonstrate how far He would go to bring men to Himself, to bring you and me to Himself. What do you feel about a God of that sort? I know what I feel. It doesn't make me feel crushed and humiliated and guilty. It makes me feel I'd do all I could for a God like that.

six

WHAT IS WORSHIP?

WELL, WHAT IS worship?

I believe everybody, unless they're frightfully self-centered, worships something or somebody. It may be a film star, a football player, a radio personality, a writer, a painter or a ballerina. It may even be, for some poor lonely soul, only the cat or the canary. But to all ordinary people there is something or somebody that calls out respect, admiration, love, and possibly wonder or even awe. All that is worship.

Listen to the crowd on the football field, cheering and yelling—and giving advice. It isn't merely the result of the match, but the physical fitness, the skill and dash of the team that are exciting admiration and enthusiasm and affection. Listen to the applause after a concert at the Albert Hall. You can almost feel the waves of admiration and gratitude and even love that flow towards those who have brought beauty and delight to the audience.

You can easily think of dozens of other examples, and when I hear clever people say that 'man has lost the capacity for

NOTE: This talk was broadcast in the People's Service on the Light Program of the B.B.C.

worship today' I disagree completely. An enormous amount
of worship is poured out every day. We may think that worship is often misdirected, or that the objects of people's worship are not worth the love and devotion given to them. We
may think, as I myself do, that it's a great pity that so little
worship is given to God. But you really can't say that people
don't worship. What you can fairly say is that most people
can't see any connection between the love and admiration
and enthusiasm that they pour out for the things or people
they are keen on and what Christians call 'worshiping God.'
I remember during the war when I was working at a
Youth Center in London, we had had a very exciting evening.
There had been a concert and dancing and speeches and
cheers and singing 'for he's a jolly good fellow' and all the
rest of it. When it came to closing time I suggested to the
leaders that we should close, as we usually did, with Club
prayers. I think I must have used the word 'worship,' for one
of them said to me quite bluntly, 'You know, we haven't any
idea what you really mean by worship!' 'Haven't you?' I
said. 'Well, it's *three cheers for God!*' That's crude, of course,
but some of those young things saw for the first time what
worship meant, or at least so they told me afterwards. They'd
spent almost the whole evening clapping and cheering people. Worship meant that they were going to acknowledge
that God was the Source of all that was jolly and friendly
and lovable in people. Worship meant that they would try
and give to Him, the Power behind 'the whole show,' the
love and admiration and respect that they were so ready to
give to human beings. Some of them, at least, saw the point.
But naturally you won't want to worship God unless you've
got an adequate idea of Him. That's why I made such a fuss,
a fortnight ago, about having a 'big enough' God in your
mind. If you've only got some half-remembered image of

God, a sort of leftover from childhood's days, there's nothing there to arouse your admiration or love or respect, and of course you won't want to worship. It's about as silly as trying to work up love for the battered old Teddy bear that you used to take to bed with you every night when you were a kid! You won't even want to give 'three cheers for God' (in the crude phrase I used) until you've seen how vast and wise, and yet how unbelievably generous and lovable, God really is.

But when you've got a grown-up idea of God, when you've seen that all the skill and beauty, all the 'niceness' and kindness and humor that you love and admire in *people*, really come from God you may quite possibly see what a wonderful Person He is. If you do, I think you'll want to worship.

And you'll want to worship more still if you accept what I talked about last week—that God actually 'focused Himself' in a human being, whom we know by the name of Jesus Christ. If you really see that God is not only vast and immensely complex Wisdom, not only the blazing source of all Truth and Beauty but also very fond of us—so fond that He was willing to accept the limitations of being a human being—I don't see that you can help worshiping. Quietly and simply and without any fuss He came down to where we are, so that He might help us rise to where He is. It meant for Him a good deal of trouble and opposition, and in the end He (who was God, remember) accepted execution as a criminal—to show how far His love for us would go, and, as I said last week, to bridge the gulf between Himself and us. Again, once you really see with your eyes wide open what sort of a God that means we have to deal with you can hardly avoid saying, 'Well, if He's like that . . . I'd like to tell Him what I feel about Him, I'd like to worship Him.'

If you accept the Christian view of God we've been talking about, I think you'll find your desire to worship Him will come along two main lines.

First you'll trace to their source all the things that make you admire and love and wonder. It doesn't matter whether it's the beauty of nature, the loveliness of music or poetry, the fascinating charms of childhood, the wonder of falling in love or any other of the thousand things that move us so deeply. We shall get into the habit of connecting them up with God, and probably say a quiet 'thank you' for them.

Sometimes, when I've read a book that has really touched me, or seen a picture that has shown some fresh beauty to me, I've felt I'd give a lot to meet the author or the painter and say a personal 'thank you.' I'm pretty sure you often feel the same.

The other day, looking at some white lilac and thinking what a miracle of beauty it is, I said to myself, 'I wish I could meet the one who designed that . . .' and then, quite suddenly, I realized what I was saying! *It was God, my Father and your Father!* And I don't mind telling you that I worshiped the Supreme Artist who designed and made white lilac.

That's the sort of thing I mean. Once you accept Christ's teaching that God is our Father, hundreds of lovely and 'wonder-full' things in everyday life make you want to say how thrilled and grateful you are. You'll want to *worship*.

The second way in which you'll want to worship goes rather deeper. You remember what I said about God not being some aloof Power living in some remote Heaven but the God who came down into the thick of it as a Man? Well, when 'the penny drops,' as we say, when you actually *realize* what sort of Person God must be to come to this earth as a baby, and live and die to show how genuinely He loves us men; and when you realize, as well, that even at this moment

God is in the here and now, actually suffering and struggling with us and in us, I'm pretty certain you'll feel 'that's the kind of God I could love, that's the kind of God I want to worship.'

If I think of God as a kind of Superarchitect who planned this amazing universe from stars to atoms, I feel a bit dazed and awed, but I don't think I particularly want to love Him. It's only when I see God coming in Person into the stream of human living, when I see Him loving and cheering and healing and inspiring people not only when He was on earth in Person 1900 years ago, but *today* whenever He's given the chance, that I feel I want to love and work for and worship Him.

Once you get it, once you realize that *all the time*, even when you broke the rules or did something that you're bitterly ashamed of now, He loved you and was only waiting for the chance to get into touch with you, I think you'll want to worship too.

One of the things that really thrill me about God is His extraordinary gentleness (I don't mean softness—He's not soft—but gentleness). We're so used to people with strong personalities having a sort of ruthless drive that it takes a bit of getting over to realize that the strongest Personality of all, the eternal God, is quiet and gentle and patient in His dealing with us. It amazes me. I mean, compared with His incredible wisdom, the best of us are conceited little fatheads full of our own importance, but He never treats us like that. He always respects our little bit of independence, and our freedom to choose. The silliest little chit of a girl can, if she likes, refuse to have anything to do with God, and *He won't force His way into her life.* It may seem strange to us (in our heart of hearts we may even think it would be better if God *did* force His way into some people's hearts), but that's

the way it is. He never did, He never does, break into anyone's personality without his or her permission. Terrific and
magnificent and splendid as He is, He knocks at the door of
your heart and mine and asks if He may come in. A God who
has such respect for each personality as that makes me want
to worship. I wonder if you feel that too.

And, of course, crowds of people *have* allowed God to
come into their lives, and they have even better reasons for
worshiping Him. They still worship God for all the marvelous
things that He has done and is doing in the world around
them; they still worship God for the way He acts towards us
human beings; but now they know Him a bit, they know
what a difference He makes to them. They know what a
steadiness and purpose He has given to their lives, they
know how He can forgive and disinfect the past. Now
they know him, a little, *personally*, and are cooperating with
His plans instead of standing aloof or acting against Him,
and their hearts are pretty full of gratitude and enthusiasm.
Such people want to worship for special personal reasons,
and I am glad to say I know a good many of them.

You see, there's a real difference between knowing *about*
God and *knowing* Him. I've already suggested using our
brains and our imaginations to get a big enough idea of God,
and I've already suggested that grown-up people, who
haven't read the Gospels since they were kids, should study
them today and see what God-become-Man was like. All
that is good and necessary and may lead you to worship. But
you'll still be worshiping Someone who is not *personally*
known to you. It is not until you freely and willingly open
your personality to the Personality of Christ that God becomes real to you. But once you drop your guard and accept
quite simply the Friendship of Christ you'll find that you
begin to see for yourself that all that I, or any other Christian

preacher, have been talking about is *true*. The love and admiration and respect and gratitude that make you cheer and clap people come out with a rush *towards God*. You want to worship Him *then*, all right.

When we worship people we want to be near them, we want to be like them, we want to do all we can for them. We want to express our love and admiration in every possible way, and we quite probably give them presents.

The same is absolutely true when we have found God and want to worship Him. We want to be near Him, we want to be like Him, we want to do all we can for Him. And we want to express our love and admiration in every possible way. That is exactly what we try to do in what we call worship. Singing and praising God are like the clapping and cheering. Following the way of Jesus Christ and doing all we can for His cause and for our fellow men expresses something of our worship in action.

But how to give Him a present to express our love is a bit of a problem. How can you give God anything when He owns everything? But does He? How about that power to choose, that precious free will that He has given to every living personality and which He so greatly respects?

That is the only present we can give—ourselves, with all our powers of spirit, mind and body—willingly, freely, given because we love Him.

That is the best and the highest worship that you and I can offer, and I am sure that it is this above all that God most highly appreciates.

seven

THE HOLY SPIRIT

CHRISTIANS BELIEVE THAT the vast Power and Mind that we call 'God' did once, so to speak, focus Himself in a human being so that we, and millions like us, might have a chance of understanding what sort of Person He is. The records of what God-become-Man did and said can easily be found. They are the four 'gospels' in your New Testament, and if you accept the belief that Jesus Christ was really God expressing Himself in a human being you can easily see that those gospel records become tremendously important.

They show us, among other things, God's plan for this world—that is, the building up of a Kingdom without frontiers, class distinctions or color bar, a fellowship of *inner* loyalty, where God is the Father and all men are brothers, and where membership does *not* cease at death.

But perhaps you feel like saying: If this has been known for 1900 years where's the result? If the present mess the world is in is the harvest of centuries of Christianity, isn't it time we tried something else?

NOTE: This talk was broadcast in the People's Service on the Light Program of the B.B.C.

Look, let's get this straight. How many people, what proportion of people, do you suppose have ever tried to take the teaching of Jesus Christ seriously in any century? Your guess is as good as mine, but I should seriously doubt if it's ever been much more than a very small percentage. Most people, even if you can get them to take the trouble to learn what Jesus Christ really said, did and taught, don't *do* anything about it. So how can you be surprised that the result seems so poor? I don't believe that Christianity, the real thing, has ever failed, but I am certain that it hasn't been given a fair chance to work, by most people. It's so much easier to go your own sweet way and say that Christianity is a beautiful ideal but it won't work, than to get down to being a real Christian. And since a great many people take the line of least resistance, that's just what's happened. The results are written all over the world. But don't blame Christianity, blame people—you might even blame yourself.

But let's get back to this plan of God for us human beings. Let's suppose that we do get the old Bible down (and blow the dust off it) and read the gospels with our grown-up minds. It soon becomes plain that Jesus Christ is calling people to live *differently*. He did not go about telling people what frightful sinners they were. He did not go about telling them vaguely to be good. But He did definitely ask people to put their own self-centered view of life aside, and to follow Him. He never said, 'If you're a good-living man life will be easy for you'—nor anything like it! He said that to follow Him would be tough and difficult; He said it might mean that you'd be laughed at, persecuted or even killed, but that you'd nevertheless find a thrill, a joy and a satisfaction in helping to build this Kingdom that would make you feel it well worth while. (Of course, those aren't His actual words; I don't want to quote a lot of texts at you—but you can take it from me that's what He said.)

Thousands of people, far more perhaps than you think, have heard Him say much the same today, and they're doing their level best to follow His methods and way of living. But when they started they all found the same snag—*they couldn't do it*. That sounds crazy but it's literally true. You try it and see! There are hundreds of things that you can do without giving God a thought. You can ride a bicycle or bake a cake or dig your garden or read a book or eat your dinner without calling on God's help at all. But the moment you seriously try to live differently, according to Christ's recipe, you find you can't. With all your will power you find you haven't got it in you to live that sort of life for more than a very short time, and even then it's a rather strained sort of performance. Probably that's why so many have tried to be Christians and then given it up.

Well, what's the answer? You may be sure that Christ didn't take all the trouble to outline this plan just to make us look silly. He's not that sort of Person. No, the answer is that we need something, some inner reinforcement, a new drive and power *inside* before Christianity becomes a working proposition.

That is exactly what He promised should be available. His own Spirit, God the Holy Spirit—the name doesn't matter—is available to help us to make the change-over, and to keep us on the new level of real living. Heaven knows, that doesn't mean we become saints overnight! But it does mean that instead of throwing up Christianity as an impossible dream, we learn, little by little, to make it come true.

Last Thursday was Ascension Day, the day when the Church commemorates Christ's return into the real per-

manent world that we sometimes call 'Heaven.' Just before
He left the earth He said a rather peculiar thing to His fol-
lowers. 'It's a good thing for you, really,' He told them, 'that
I'm leaving you, for now I shall send you my Spirit who
will be with you always and everywhere.' Do you see the
point? He meant that so long as He was on this earth *as a*
Man He could be in only one place at a time. But if He came,
so to speak, as God the Spirit He could and would be any-
where He was needed and sincerely called upon to be. In
other words He was not just going to be an inspiring Figure
of the Past, but an available Power in the Present.

I want to make it quite clear that this Spirit of God is real
and personal. We often talk about things like the *spirit* of the
old school, the *spirit* of Dunkirk, the *spirit* of modern youth,
etc. But although we are talking about something more or
less definite, we are certainly not talking about a Person. But
when Christians talk about the Holy Spirit they do mean a
Person—they mean the Personality of God acting on and in
ordinary human personalities. And it is, of course, this living Spirit of God Who produces in people real Christian living. If we open our personalities to His influence we can
become real Christians—there's no other way of doing that.

Of course you can go on believing vaguely in Almighty
God, the One Above, Who is aloof from all the strains and
problems of modern living. And of course you can go on
believing that Jesus Christ lived a beautiful life 1900 years
ago, and left us a set of lovely ideals. But if you ever want
religion to become real to you, to make a difference to your
life, you will find you have to deal with the Living Spirit of
God here and now—in other words, with God the Holy
Spirit.

Now of course all this is so much theological moonshine
unless it actually works in practice.

I believe it does. Here's a simple example. If you are writing a poem and the rhymes won't come or the lines won't fit you may cry, 'Oh, William Shakespeare, help me!' and nothing whatever happens. If you're feeling jittery you may think of some hero of the past, like Nelson, and say, 'Oh, Horatio Nelson, help me!' But again there isn't the slightest response. But if you're trying to lead a Christian life and realize you're coming to the end of your own moral strength and you cry, 'Oh, Christ, help me!' something does happen, at once, just like that. There is a living Spirit immediately available, and millions have proved His existence.

But I'm not only thinking, of course, of the sudden emergency. I'm thinking of the effect of the continual contact of God's Spirit on a human personality. I mean, suppose a man over a period of years deliberately welcomes God's Spirit. He'll do it by prayer and worship, of course, and by living as nearly as he can the sort of life Jesus Christ lived. What sort of result would you expect to see?

I'm going to let someone else answer that one—a man who lived in the days when Christianity first got going. We've still got what he wrote as a result of actually seeing this Spirit of God working in ordinary people like you and me. (It's in your New Testament, by the way—Paul's Epistle to the Galatians, chapter five, verse twenty-two.) This is what he wrote: 'The fruit of the Spirit is love, joy, peace, patience, gentleness, goodness, faith, adaptability and self-control.'

Now Paul was no wishful thinker: he wasn't that kind of person at all. He was writing about what he'd actually observed in some of the early Christians. Some of them had been pretty tough eggs, even for those days, before they became Christians, believe me! Not that that worried a man like Paul. He knew, from his own experience, that if once a man would 'open up' to God, the fruit of love, joy, peace, goodness and all the rest would begin to replace all the rotten things that had been there before. Of course he'd known a lot of people *refuse* to let it happen, but he'd seen the change often enough to be able to give us in detail the sort of 'fruit' the Spirit of God produces in human life.

Our trouble is not that we don't like that list of virtues—love, joy, peace, etc.—in fact, we know jolly well that they're the very things the world is so terribly short of. No, our trouble is that many of us don't really believe that there is a living Spirit of God capable of making, and maintaining, any fundamental change in our lives. Perhaps we think of people as just 'types'—good types, poor types, glamorous types, hardworking types and all the rest, and in our heart of hearts we don't really think anything much can be done about it.

The Christian faith denies that pessimistic belief completely! Every time we say, 'I believe in the Holy Spirit,' we mean that we believe that there is a living God able and willing to enter human personality, and change it. It may take a long time, but it's possible, possible to anyone who'll honestly give God a chance.

Now, don't get me wrong. There's a certain amount of truth in that 'type' business, of course, and however sincerely you make contact with the Spirit of God you will not suddenly find yourself endowed with a good head for figures, or a gift for organization if these are not in your make-up already. The difference will be made in the *direction* of your life, and the change will be in the *quality* of your living. You will find yourself becoming much more at peace within yourself, you will find yourself taking much more interest in other people. God will be more real to you, and worshiping and serving Him will, perhaps quite suddenly, make sense to you. *You* may not be conscious that you've become easier to live with, but other people will! The love, joy, peace, gentleness, faith and all the other virtues Paul talked of will be produced in you, and yet you'll still be *you*. Marvelous, isn't it? And yet it's true. I've seen it happen, not perhaps so dramatically as Paul did, but just as genuinely.

We all want a better world, but you can't have a better world without better people. For better people you need ideals and faith, but you need more than that. You need a *Spirit* to make the whole thing work, not just a flash of inspiration but a steady, living, transforming Spirit.

And that is just what has been given to us—God, the Holy Spirit.

~ eight

A THING MOST WONDERFUL

A FEW YEARS ago on Good Friday one of my choirboys said
to me, 'Sir, why ever do they call this *Good* Friday?' I think
that was a very sensible question to ask. For after all, what
we are remembering today seems very far from good. For we
shall be thinking of the painful and public death of a young
man by the name of Jesus Christ. The Crucifixion certainly
was not good for Him, but as Christians we believe that that
Young Man who died upon the Cross did something good
for us men. He reconciled us to God. So, although we cannot
be particularly cheerful on a day when we are remembering
something that was so deeply tragic, yet we can and do
thank God that it was a good thing that He did. Good for us
and good for all men, even though the doing of it cost Him
so much. Believing as Christians do that the young man was
God in human form, we are bound to feel a little overawed
by the thought of how far He was willing to go to win us to
Himself.

Today Christians all over the world are thinking in imagination of that figure of a young man dying upon the Cross.

NOTE: This talk was broadcast in the Overseas Service of the B.B.C.

It is, of course, only too easy to see the tragic injustice of it, and anyone who is at all sensitive can readily feel what a dreadful thing it was to have happened. But I think we want to be realistic and definite about what it is we are looking at. We are seeing, not just the cruel death of an innocent young man at the hands of the wicked and unscrupulous—after all, that kind of thing has happened a good many times in this sorry world—but we are looking at something that is, strange though it seems, a deliberate Act of God. You see, even before the tragedy itself, when it was obvious to Jesus Christ what was going to happen, He spoke of the necessity of His Death as part of a Divine Plan. The disciples at the time, and especially Peter, found it hard to understand, and it seemed to them that, as the plotting of wicked men closed in upon their Friend and Master, discretion would have been far the better part of valor. But Jesus Himself did not see it like that, and He rebuked Peter sternly for avoiding the real issue. He went on deliberately and with His eyes wide open to what He knew would mean a shameful and degrading death.

It is plain from the Gospel story that Jesus regarded His own approaching death as a bitter necessity. Yet we, like the disciples who 'followed with fear in their hearts,' as the Gospel tells us, may well feel puzzled as they. Why must the One whom they were beginning to recognize as God-in-human-form undergo such a frightful death? Surely, if ever, this was a case for divine intervention, for the flashing down of the celestial army of rescue that men might know who had been in their midst. Yet nothing of the kind occurred. The travesty of justice took its course, and the Man who was God in human form was brutally flogged and nailed to a wooden cross to die in the blazing sun.

We can appreciate the heroism and we can feel something

of the tragedy, but can we understand the necessity, the bitter necessity?

I think, in order to do this, we have to think a little of the nature of God and of man. So long as we are skirting round the edges of the Christian Faith, thinking of God as some vague distant Benevolence, we shall not see the clamant need for reconciliation between God and man. But once we attempt with our adult minds and hearts to lead a Christian life, we begin to see the difficulty. For the gulf between us and God is not merely an intellectual one—it is not that God is infinitely wise and we, by comparison, blundering fools, though that is true—but the real gulf lies in the moral realm. You and I, through our own sins and failures, as well as by the infection of the sins of other people, are separated from God by a moral gulf. All serious religions recognize this, and all of them attempt some bridgehead from sinful human nature towards the Beauty and Perfection of the Holiness of God. Yes, they all attempt bridgeheads, but just as it is impossible to build a bridge across a chasm without starting from both sides, so it proves impossible in this matter of a moral gulf to do more than erect a painful and desperate bridgehead, *unless Someone is also building from the other side.* And that is precisely what we believe Christ did for us men. Not only did He, who was by nature God, come down to be born as a human being, not only did He live a life of perfect sinlessness, not only did He give us the 'blueprint' or 'recipe' for happy and constructive living, but in Himself He built the Bridge to span the gulf between God and man. 'God was in Christ reconciling the world unto Himself.'

The whole of mankind is caught up in a vicious circle of sin, suffering and death, and Jesus Christ, Himself God and Himself Man, deliberately allowed Himself to be caught up in that deadly process. Though personally He had never done anything but good, though personally He had had no dealings with any form of sin, He, as Representative Man (for that is what 'Son of Man' means), took the rap for mankind. We cannot begin to understand what kind of horror and revulsion such an experience must have meant to Him. It was, of course, not merely the physical degradation and suffering, but the terrifying dark experience of allowing evil to close in upon Him and kill Him, that fills us with wonder and awe.

In all our minds, sometimes lurking deep beneath the conscious level, there lies a sense that there is this gulf between us and God, and that something ought to be done about it. We make our good resolutions, we turn over new leaves—or we try to laugh the whole thing off—but there remains the sense that we are a long way from God and that there is nothing that we can do to close the gap. Sometimes we feel a passing sympathy with those heathen religions which make sacrifices, or go through complicated rituals of atonement to make themselves right with God, but we of the twentieth century feel we have grown beyond that sort of thing, though we have not grown beyond the sense that something ought to be done to atone for our sins and failures.

When we look at the Cross, without sentimentality, but with a little thought and imagination, we realize that what we could never do, what we are always powerless to do, *has been done*, by Christ. This is the Act of Reconciliation which we could never make, the Bridge which we could never build. No longer do we see God as the Fearful Judge isolated in splendid Majesty, but right down among us, taking upon Him our flesh and plunging into the heart of our insoluble difficulty. When we see what sort of a God the Cross reveals to us, it is no exaggeration to say that a revolution takes place in our thinking and our feeling. It is not too difficult to hurl defiance at a high and mighty God who, secure in His majesty, makes us mortals feel guilty and afraid. But it is impossible to be unmoved when we see our very Creator down in the sweat and dust of the arena, going to that awe-inspiring length to make the Reconciliation. It may come quietly into our hearts, or it may break over us like a wave, that the nature of God is not, as we supposed, that of a Tyrant, a Spoilsport, or a Jesting Fate, but Love—not sentimental love, but real Love, that would face the grim degradation of the Cross to reconcile us to Himself.

nine

THE FIRST PORTRAIT OF JESUS

EVERYONE KNOWS THE story of the Roman Emperor Nero playing the fiddle while Rome was burning. Whether that's true or not, we can't be sure, but we do know that there was a great fire in Rome in the winter of A.D. 64–65 and that Nero tried to put the blame for it on the Christians. It was soon after this time that what is, as far as we know, the first written biography of Jesus Christ appeared. It was written by John Mark, himself a native of Jerusalem, and there is pretty good evidence for believing that much of the material that Mark recorded came from what Peter remembered.

The book which nowadays is usually known as the 'Gospel according to St. Mark' is quite a short one, for in those days they didn't go in for full-length biographies. Its style is vivid, and there are no decorations. Mark sets out to put down the plain facts, and from his simply told story there emerges a strong portrait of Jesus. Many people, of course, have read Mark's Gospel more than once in English, but not so many will have read it in detail again and again in the original Greek, which is what a translator has to do. If you had done

NOTE: This talk was broadcast in the Home Service of the B.B.C.

that, you would find that Mark is nothing like so simple and naïve as he at first appears. I don't know whether he was conscious of being an artist or not, but I do know that the strong lines of his work produce a bold and unforgettable portrait which comes alive from the simple sentences that he wrote. I should like to pass on to you some of the impressions of Jesus Christ which a close study of Mark's Gospel produced in my own mind.

I find no trace at all in Mark's Gospel of 'gentle Jesus meek and mild'! I find instead a most powerful Figure who moves with confidence, cheerfulness and courage. He is a Man plainly in touch with the unseen world and plainly conscious that, though fully human, He speaks with the authority of God Himself. You remember the story of the four men who were determined to get their paralysed friend within reach of Jesus' power of healing? Jesus makes, as far as we can judge, an instantaneous diagnosis, and says to the paralytic, 'My son, your sins are forgiven.' There is no suggestion of arrogance here, but simply of authority. But of course the religious leaders who happened to be present were furious with a mere man who dared to forgive sins. Here is Mark's account of Jesus' reaction to that.

Jesus realised instantly what they were thinking, and said to them,

'Why must you argue like this in your minds? Which do you suppose is easier—to say to a paralysed man, "Your sins are forgiven," or "Get up, pick up your mat and walk"? But to prove to you that the Son of Man has full authority to forgive sins on earth, I say to you,'—and here he spoke to the paralytic—'Get up, pick up your mat and go home.'

At once the man sprang to his feet, picked up his mat and walked off in full view of them all. Everyone was amazed, praised God, and said,

'We have never seen anything like this before.'

Then again, when Jesus healed the man with the shriveled hand in the Synagogue on the Sabbath day, or as we might say, 'in Church on Sunday,' Mark says: 'He looked round *in anger* at the faces surrounding him.' He was really angry that men could be so utterly callous as to think that the sanctity of the Sabbath could possibly be more important than the healing of a human being. Not for one second do you get the impression that Jesus doubted that He Himself was right and that His opponents were blasphemously wrong.

Then I like the human touch of Jesus' own family circle who had doubtless heard about His preaching and healing and defying the religious authorities. 'They set out,' Mark writes, 'to take charge of him, for they said, "He must be mad!"' Yet the Figure who springs alive from those pages is always poised and balanced. Immediately after His family's fears for His sanity, Mark records another remark of Jesus which I imagine was spoken with a cheerful smile to show how laughable was the charge that He did His miracles of healing because He was in league with the Devil.

'How can Satan be the one who drives out Satan? If a kingdom is divided against itself, then that kingdom cannot last, and if a household is divided against itself, it cannot last either. And if Satan leads a rebellion against Satan—his days are certainly numbered.'

You can imagine how sheepish some at least of His opponents must have felt at such downright common sense. But this courageous, confident Son of Man can be very gentle and sympathetic when the occasion demands it. Do you remember Jairus, the Synagogue president, and how he sent an urgent message to Jesus to say that his daughter was dying? Jesus began to come to his house, but on the way there was what must have been for the frantic father a most maddening interruption. The woman with the internal haemorrhage must choose this moment to try to touch Jesus, and, oh dear, He must stop and find out who did so! We can imagine Jairus praying under his breath, 'Oh, hurry, hurry!' And then it seems too late. The fatal message comes: 'Your daughter is dead . . . there is no need to bother the Master any further.' Then Mark records Jesus' calm and reassuring words to Jairus, 'Now, don't be afraid, just go on believing.'

Then, with no sympathy at all for the hired mourners and neighbors whom He found weeping and wailing in the house where the girl lay apparently dead, He turns them all out and says tenderly in Aramaic, 'Wake up, little girl!' Of course the parents went nearly out of their minds with joy. We can imagine the hugging and the kissing that went on. Mark does not record this, but he does record that Jesus, practical as ever, suggested that she might be given something to eat!

I think it is difficult for us to understand the courage shown by Jesus when He dared to challenge the authority of the Scribes and Pharisees. There is no body of people today, at any rate in our own country, surrounded by such apparently divine authority, and living on such a pinnacle of prestige and privilege. Jesus does not merely defy them, but exposes their hypocrisy and shows the absurdity of their treasured traditions. Listen to Mark's record of one of these clashes with the religious authorities.

'It is wonderful to see how you can set aside the Commandment of God to preserve your own tradition! For Moses said, *"Honour thy father and thy mother"* and *"He that speaketh evil of father or mother, let him die the death."* But you say, if a man says to his father or his mother, Korban—meaning, "I have given God whatever duty I owed to you," then he need not lift a finger any longer for his father or mother, so making the Word of God

invalid for the sake of the tradition which you hold. And this is
typical of much of what you do.'

I sometimes think the solemn majesty of the Authorized
Version blinds us to the warm humanity, yes, and the humor
of the words of Jesus. How aloof and solemn does His reply to
the Syrophoenician woman sound in the Authorized Version:
'Let the children first be filled, for it is not meet to take the
children's bread and to cast it unto the dogs.' But suppose it
was said with a kind of dry humor or even with a twinkle in
the eye, as Mark's language seems to me to imply, Jesus'
words sound quite different:

'You must let the children have all they want first. It is not
right, you know, to take the children's food and throw it to the
dogs.'
But she replied,
'Yes, Lord, I know, but even the dogs under the table eat what
the children leave.'
'If you can answer like that,' Jesus replied, 'you can go home!
The evil spirit has left your daughter.'

The Man who moves with such confidence in the pages of
Mark's story is plainly One to whom the resources of God are
always available. When He was in His own village He re-
marked with perhaps a wry smile, 'No prophet goes unhon-
oured—except in his own country or with his own relations or
in his own home! And he could do nothing miraculous there
apart from laying his hands on a few sick people and healing
them; their lack of faith astonished him.' Then later on, when
the disciples failed to heal the epileptic boy, Mark records a
very human impatience on the part of Jesus:

'Oh, what a faithless people you are! How long must I be with
you before you will believe; how long must I bear your lack of
faith? Bring him here to me.'

And when the father of the boy bursts out: 'But if you can do anything, please take pity on us and help us,' Jesus retorts:

'If *I* can do anything! Everything is possible to the man who believes.'

Indeed it must have seemed astonishing to Jesus Who was, so to speak, completely open on the God-ward side, to see men so blind to the possibilities of what God could do.

The early pages of Mark record almost a triumphal progress. Enthusiastic crowds followed Him everywhere. The disciples, I think we might fairly guess, very much enjoyed their share in the work and it was probably a gay company who followed Him from triumph to triumph. But Jesus knew perfectly well that bitter hostility was growing against Him and that it was inevitable that He should go through much suffering and be killed. Mark records that He told the disciples this 'quite bluntly.' Peter voiced the objections of the others who saw no reason why their hero should run deliberately into danger and was sharply rebuked by Jesus. But when the actual moment came for Jesus to take the road to Jerusalem for the last time, they made no attempt to dissuade Him.

'Jesus walked on ahead,' Mark records. 'They were puzzled and bewildered at this, but went on following Him, with fear in their hearts.'

It is easy for us to be wise after the event, but I like Mark's economical comment that they went on following Him despite the fear in their hearts. Now although Jesus knew that He was going to Jerusalem to His death, the net did not close around Him immediately. He is in the heart of things now, the heart of worship and authority. He is Reality, Truth and Love in the very center of unreality and bitter hatred. But although by now He knows that His death is inescapable, He still speaks the truth with devastating wit. Mark records Him saying, in the lion's mouth, so to speak,

'Be on your guard against these Scribes who love to walk about in long robes and to be greeted respectfully in public and to have the front seats in the synagogue and the best places at dinner-parties! These are the men who live on widows' property and then put up a screen of lengthy prayers.'

He is not so strained and harassed that He fails to notice the widow's tiny gift into the Temple treasury. He comments:

'Believe me, this poor widow has put in more than all the others. For they have all put in what they can easily spare, but she in her poverty who needs so much, has given away everything, her whole living!'

Nor does He fail in generous appreciation of the woman who saw that He had to die and anointed Him with a costly gift.

Vividly too there stands out in my recollection the gentleness of Jesus, Himself racked almost beyond enduring in the agony of the Garden, towards the weakness of others.

Then he came and found them fast asleep. He spoke to Peter, 'Are you asleep, Simon? Couldn't you manage to watch for a single hour? Watch and pray, all of you, that you may not have to face temptation. Your spirit is willing, but human nature is weak.'

Even at the betrayal I see nothing meek and mild about the attitude of Jesus. Indeed, He meets the arresting party with blazing scorn:

'So you've come out with your swords and staves to capture me like a bandit, have you? Day after day I was with you in the

Temple teaching, and you never laid a finger on me. But the Scriptures must be fulfilled.'

The final scenes of Jesus' earthly life Mark describes briefly and without comment. The Man is deserted by His friends and completely in the power of His deadly enemies. For the most part He maintains a dignified silence. But when He is faced with the direct question, 'Are you Christ?' He replies, 'I am! Yes, you will see the Son of Man sitting at the right hand of power, coming in the clouds of heaven.' He is still sure of who He is. Not that that spares Him the sort of humiliation that we might think would be impossible in any Court of Law. But Mark records:

And their verdict was that he deserved to die. Then some of them began to spit at him. They bindfolded him and then slapped him, saying,
  'Now prophesy who hit you!'
Even the servants who took him away slapped his face.

At the Cross itself the leaders of religion, who should surely have had some sense of decency and human dignity, made fun of Him among themselves, and even the men who were crucified with Him hurled abuse at Him. It remained for a pagan, a Roman centurion, to pay the only tribute, and Mark says briefly: 'When the centurion who stood in front of Jesus saw how he died, he said, "He must indeed have been a son of God!"' . . . probably the highest tribute a pagan soldier could pay to a brave man.

It is the women, says St. Mark, who didn't desert Him at the end, and who watched the final dreadful scene. It is the women who very early on the day after the sabbath came to the tomb to make the body as decent as possible in death, according to their custom. They encountered the 'young man in white' who tells them that Jesus is no longer there, but has risen as He said He would. And Mark's Gospel ends with short, almost gasping, sentences: 'And they got out of the tomb and ran away from it. They were trembling with excitement. They did not dare to breathe a word to anyone.'

It's pretty certain that what we now find tacked on to the end of Mark's Gospel is not Mark's work at all. Perhaps he meant to end on that note of breathless awe and astonishment, for the people for whom he was writing knew very well that Jesus was alive. In A.D. 65 Christianity had not become formalized; it was a matter of loyalty to a living Person on the one hand, and the dependable, demonstrable power of that Person on the other. In the intense life of the early Church, surrounded as they were by bitter persecution, and often by the threat of martyrdom, the living presence of the living Christ was a day-by-day reality.

May I beg you to read Mark's work again? It is not long, and if you read it in one of the several good modern versions you will get away from merely traditional reverence, and see for yourself the truth of what I have been saying. Read it, more than once if you can, with as open a mind as possible, and let the strong lines of this narrative build up for you, as they did for me, a vigorous portrait of One who is a matchless Man. When you see for yourself the stature and quality of the Man, it will not seem to you nearly so difficult to accept what Christians have always accepted—that the Son of Man was also the Son of God.